STECK-VAUGHN
PORTRAIT OF AMERICA

South Dakota

Copyright © 1996 Steck-Vaughn Company

Steck-Vaughn Company

Executive Editor	Diane Sharpe
Senior Editor	Martin S. Saiewitz
Design Manager	Pamela Heaney
Photo Editor	Margie Foster

Proof Positive/Farrowlyne Associates, Inc.
Program Editorial, Revision Development, Design, and Production

Consultant: Nancy T. Koupal, Research and Publishing, South Dakota State Historical Society

Published by Raintree Steck-Vaughn Publishers, an imprint of Steck-Vaughn Company.

A Turner Educational Services, Inc. book. Based on the Portrait of America television series by R. E. (Ted) Turner.

Cover Photo: Mount Rushmore National Monument by © Dick Dietrich/FPG International.

Library of Congress Cataloging-in-Publication Data

Thompson, Kathleen.
    South Dakota / Kathleen Thompson.
       p.   cm. — (Portrait of America)
    "A Turner book."
    "Based on the Portrait of America television series"—T.p. verso.
    Includes index.
    ISBN 0-8114-7387-2 (library binding).—ISBN 0-8114-7468-2 (softcover)
    1. South Dakota—Juvenile literature. I. Title. II. Series:
Thompson, Kathleen. Portrait of America.
F651.3.T48 1996
978.3—dc20
                             95-25722
                             CIP
                             AC

Printed and Bound in the United States of America

1 2 3 4 5 6 7 8 9 10 WZ 98 97 96 95

Acknowledgments
The publishers wish to thank the following for permission to reproduce photographs:
P. 7 © Chad Coppess/South Dakota Tourism; p. 8 The Mammoth Site of Hot Springs, South Dakota, Inc.; p. 10 (both) © Mark Kayser/South Dakota Tourism; p. 12 National Portrait Gallery, Smithsonian Institution; p. 13 Wyoming State Archives, Museums and Historical Department; pp. 14, 15, 16 South Dakota Historical Society; p. 17 (both) © Chad Coppess/South Dakota Tourism; p. 18 South Dakota Department of Game, Fish, and Parks; p. 19 AP/Wide World; pp. 20, 21 Rushmore Borglum Story; p. 22 (top) © Hal Sommer, (bottom) Rushmore Borglum Story; p. 23 Rushmore Borglum Story; p. 24 South Dakota Tourism; p. 26 (both) © Chad Coppess/South Dakota Tourism; p. 27 South Dakota Tourism; p. 28 (top) South Dakota Tourism, (bottom) © Chad Coppess/South Dakota Tourism; pp. 29, 30 South Dakota Tourism; pp. 31 (both), 32 © Chad Coppess/South Dakota Tourism; p. 34 South Dakota Tourism; p. 35 (top) South Dakota Tourism, (bottom) South Dakota Art Museum Collection, Brooklings, South Dakota; pp. 36 (both), 37 © Chad Coppess/South Dakota Tourism; p. 38 Crazy Horse Memorial Archive; pp. 39, 40, 41© Robb De Wall/Crazy Horse Memorial; p. 42 © Chuck Pefley/Tony Stone Images; p. 44 South Dakota Tourism; p. 46 One Mile Up; p. 47 (left) One Mile Up, (center, right) South Dakota Tourism.

STECK-VAUGHN
PORTRAIT OF AMERICA

South Dakota

Kathleen Thompson

A Turner Book

RSVP

**RAINTREE
STECK-VAUGHN**
P U B L I S H E R S
The Steck-Vaughn Company

Austin, Texas

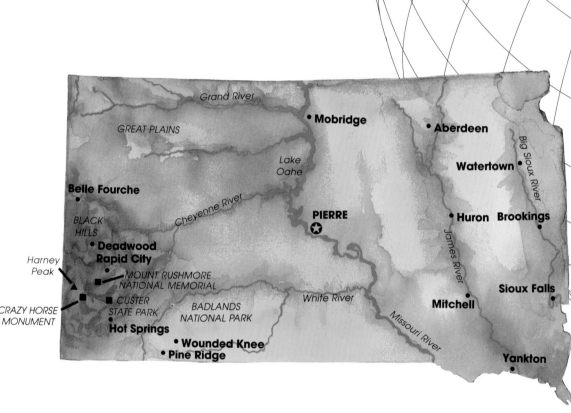

South Dakota

Grand River

GREAT PLAINS

• Mobridge

• Aberdeen

Lake
Oahe

Watertown

Big Sioux River

Belle Fourche

BLACK
HILLS

Cheyenne River

PIERRE
⭐

• Huron Brookings

Harney
Peak

Deadwood
Rapid City

MOUNT RUSHMORE
NATIONAL MEMORIAL

James River

CRAZY HORSE
MONUMENT

CUSTER
STATE PARK

BADLANDS
NATIONAL PARK

White River

Sioux Falls

Hot Springs

Mitchell

Missouri River

• Wounded Knee
• Pine Ridge

Yankton

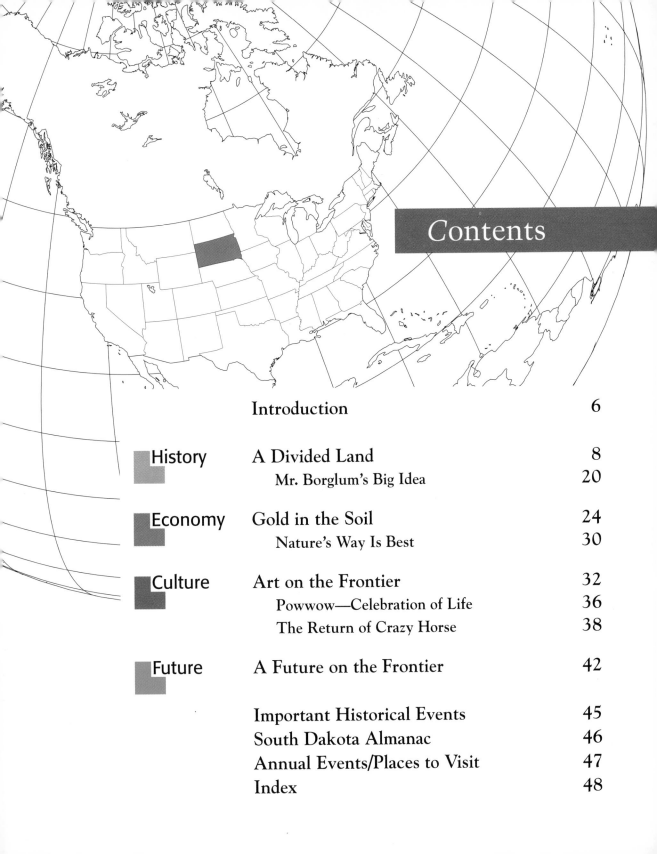

Contents

Introduction

South Dakota, often called the Land of Infinite Variety, presents a landscape of extremes. It is split by the Missouri River flowing south past the capital city of Pierre. Crystal-clear lakes and lush croplands lie to the east. To the west are deep canyons, the windswept Badlands, and the Black Hills. The richest gold mines in the Western Hemisphere are buried in these hills.

A variety of interesting people have shaped the history of South Dakota. Adventurous explorers, proud Native Americans, determined farmers, and resourceful gold miners made their mark on the state. Today, South Dakota's people remain as colorful and fascinating as the landscape and history of the state itself.

Sunflowers thrive in South Dakota's sunshine.

South Dakota

farming, gold, buffalo

A Divided Land

Archaeologists have found evidence of civilizations in present-day South Dakota from as early as 8000 B.C. Many artifacts have been found along the Missouri River in the center of the state, and in the Black Hills in the western part. Evidence shows that these early inhabitants hunted, fished, and ate berries and roots gathered from the forests and prairies.

A group known today as the Mound Builders lived along the Missouri River from around A.D. 500. They constructed huge earthen mounds that they used as burial sites. Other mounds were used for religious ceremonies. The Mound Builders vanished three hundred years after they arrived. No one is sure why they disappeared, but some archaeologists believe that disease may have been the cause.

Descendants of the Mound Builders, the Arikara, lived in northern-central South Dakota in the 1500s. They grew corn, which they traded with other Native American groups for clothing and meat. The Arikara also hunted elk, deer, and buffalo. By the 1700s, when

During the Ice Age, about one hundred woolly mammoths perished after becoming trapped in this spot. Twenty-six thousand years later, these archaeologists at Hot Springs are carefully unearthing the mammoth bones.

Native Americans hunted buffalo, mostly for food and clothing. Some carved the bones into tools, used the skulls for ceremonies, or turned parts of muscle into thread and strings for hunting bows.

An average buffalo stands about six feet high and weighs 1,800 pounds but can still outrun a horse!

Europeans were first beginning to explore the area, there were nearly four thousand Arikara living there.

The Cheyenne moved from present-day Minnesota to the central South Dakota region near the Arikara in the 1700s. Later they moved to the Black Hills in western South Dakota. The Cheyenne carried on a nomadic, or wandering, lifestyle. They lived in teepees, which they could take apart and carry with them as they moved across the Plains. The Cheyenne were dependent on their horses to help them keep up with the migrations of the buffalo herds. Besides hunting the buffalo for its meat, they used the skin for clothing, blankets, and as covering for the teepees.

In 1682 the French had claimed all of the land reached by the Mississippi River and its branches, including the South Dakota region. They called the area Louisiana in honor of King Louis XIV. In 1743 French-Canadian brothers François and Joseph La Vérendrye explored the territory for France. A few French traders followed and exchanged tools and other items with the Native Americans for furs. Few of these French traders tried to settle in the area permanently.

The Sioux, who included the Lakota, Nakota, and Dakota peoples, arrived in the area around the mid-1700s. They left their homeland in present-day Minnesota when they were forced out by other Native American groups. These groups had all come to Minnesota after being driven out of their eastern homelands by settlers. The Sioux, who had been mainly an agricultural people, changed their lifestyle in South Dakota. They lived like the Cheyenne, following the buffalo herds and living in temporary settlements.

By about 1800 the Sioux had pushed most of the Cheyenne and the Arikara out of South Dakota. The Sioux occupied a broad strip of land east of the Rocky Mountains that included parts of present-day North Dakota, Kansas, and Nebraska, in addition to most of western South Dakota.

In 1803 the United States bought the entire Louisiana Territory from the French. President Thomas Jefferson sent the explorers Meriwether Lewis and William Clark to explore the country's new purchase. The Lewis and Clark expedition spent about seven weeks in the South Dakota area before heading north and west. Their reports attracted American fur traders to the South Dakota area.

The fur trade prospered with the establishment of trading posts such as Fort La Framboise in 1817. To be successful, these traders needed to keep relations with the Native Americans friendly. For a while traders and Native Americans lived in peace.

But this peace didn't last. In 1823 the Arikara tried to block a trading party traveling up the Missouri River and killed 13 traders. The United States cavalry was sent to force the Native Americans northward.

In 1859 one of the first permanent European settlements in the area was established at Yankton. The rich farmland of the eastern South Dakota area began to attract more farmers than traders. Settlements were established mainly along the Missouri River and its tributaries. In 1861 President James Buchanan approved the creation of the Dakota Territory as part of the United States. Yankton became the capital. The territory included all of what is now North and South Dakota in addition to large parts of Montana and Wyoming. Less than five thousand settlers and fur traders lived in this entire region.

Native Americans and the United States Army fought a series of battles during the 1860s. The largest conflict was known as Red Cloud's War. It began when gold was discovered in Montana to the west of the territory. To reach the goldfields of Montana, the United States government began building a road called the Bozeman Trail through the heart of the Sioux hunting grounds. Red Cloud, chief of the Oglala Sioux, kept up regular attacks on the American troops

Red Cloud was the Sioux leader of the raids that stopped construction of the Bozeman Trail. Later in his life, Red Cloud often traveled to Washington, D.C., to criticize the government's treatment of Native Americans.

sent to guard workers on the trail. Finally, in 1867 the government halted construction. One year later the Sioux and the United States government signed the Fort Laramie Treaty of 1868, in which the government gave up building the Bozeman Trail. The treaty also promised all of South Dakota west of the Missouri River to the Sioux.

In 1874 the government sent Lieutenant Colonel George A. Custer to the Sioux reservation to make sure that settlers respected the Fort Laramie Treaty. The government also wanted to investigate reports of gold found in the Black Hills, which were part of the reservation. They soon discovered the reports were true. In 1875 the Black Hills gold rush was in full force.

Custer and his troops tried to keep miners off the Sioux reservation, but the miners were stubborn. The government then tried to negotiate with the Sioux to buy the land for over five million dollars. But the Sioux had made the Black Hills sacred hunting grounds, so they refused the government's offer.

Government leaders then stopped trying to keep the miners out and started trying to remove the Sioux instead. As miners trekked into the sacred grounds, the Sioux gathered to stop them.

In the spring of 1876, Sioux leaders Rain-in-the-Face, Crazy Horse, and Sitting Bull led raids against the miners and battled the American soldiers in Montana, Wyoming, and South Dakota. Some of these battles were well publicized, especially the massacre of Custer's regiment at the Little Bighorn in Montana.

Before Lieutenant Colonel George Custer came to the Black Hills, he had fought for the Union in the Civil War.

Most of the public reaction at this time was against the Native Americans. By 1877 the Sioux were thoroughly defeated. They were forced to give up their claim to the Black Hills. Red Cloud summed up the relationship between Native Americans and the United States government with these words: "They made us many promises, more than I remember, but they never kept but one; they promised to take our land, and they took it."

People swarmed into the Black Hills seeking gold. Mining towns, such as Deadwood and Lead, were established to serve the population boom. Many others came to the territory to farm and to raise sheep and cattle. Settlement in the territory increased with the coming of railroad lines, beginning around 1880. In about ten years, the population of South Dakota more than quadrupled, reaching 325,000 in the late 1880s.

In the 1870s, Deadwood had a reputation for being one of the wildest towns on the frontier. Wild Bill Hickock and Calamity Jane were two of its most famous residents.

This family is sitting outside their homestead. Between 1878 and 1887, settlers flocked to South Dakota to take advantage of the federal government's sale of more than 24 million acres of land.

Dakota settlers petitioned the United States government for statehood.

The Dakota Territory was now much smaller than when it had been created. The Montana Territory had been carved out of it in 1864, and the Wyoming Territory had been separated from it in 1868. In 1889 Congress divided the remaining territory across the middle. That November, North and South Dakota entered the Union at the same time. Alphabetical order determined North Dakota as the thirty-ninth state and South Dakota as the fortieth.

In 1890 the Sioux began performing rituals called the Ghost Dances. Native Americans believed that the Ghost Dances would cause the buffalo to come back and the American settlers to be destroyed.

The United States government, afraid that the Ghost Dances would lead to another Native American

Sitting Bull united the Sioux across the Great Plains in their struggles to retain their land.

uprising, outlawed the ritual. The Sioux refused to stop, however, and in the resulting violence Sitting Bull and many other Native Americans were killed.

About one hundred of Sitting Bull's followers then fled to join Big Foot's band on the Cheyenne River. The whole group moved farther south to seek shelter with other Ghost Dancers in the Badlands, southeast of the Black Hills. The Seventh Cavalry, Custer's old regiment, caught up with Big Foot's band and ordered the group to camp at Wounded Knee Creek. The next morning the soldiers began to collect all the weapons from the Sioux. One of the weapons was accidentally fired. The soldiers immediately opened fire with machine guns, shooting everyone in their path. About two hundred men, women, and children never had a chance; many were killed before they could run. The rest were chased down and shot. The Wounded Knee massacre devastated not only the Sioux but all Native Americans as the news reached them. The incident was the last major Native American battle.

Almost one hundred thousand new settlers moved onto the former Sioux reservation in western South Dakota between 1900 and 1910. The population boom slowed down in 1911 when a major drought fell upon the state.

South Dakota's economy received a boost when the United States entered World War I in 1917. All of the state's farming and ranching products were needed to feed the soldiers overseas. When the war ended in 1918, however, the demand for South Dakota farm products returned to normal. At about this time, the state entered a number of commercial businesses. The most successful of these was the South Dakota Cement Commission plant at Rapid City.

The 1930s was a time of extreme hardship for the people of South Dakota. First, the Great Depression brought a severe economic decline. Millions of people all over the United States were out of work. Banks and businesses closed their doors. Then, from 1933 to 1934 another severe drought—the worst in the state's history—and a plague of crop-eating grasshoppers wiped out nearly four thousand farms.

President Franklin D. Roosevelt took office in 1933, at the height of the Depression. He developed public works projects all over the country to create jobs. In South Dakota, people in this program went to work creating new roads, bridges, and recreation areas in the Black Hills. The government also provided help

Red Cloud's grave is honored at the Red Cloud Heritage Center, near Wounded Knee.

Custer State Park was first created by the South Dakota legislature in 1919. Since then it has grown from 48,000 to 73,000 acres.

The Hayes Lake Spillway is one of the many projects that put people to work during the Great Depression. A spillway drains water along the sides of a dam when the level of the reservoir behind it gets too high.

to farmers in planting new kinds of wheat that could survive long dry periods. The government also raised the price of gold. This made gold mining profitable enough for miners to go back to work.

When the United States entered World War II in 1941, South Dakota's farms once again were valuable in providing food for troops overseas. The state's farmers used modern methods and machinery that helped produce record-breaking crops. Unfortunately these machines took the place of many workers. In 1944 the federal government approved the Missouri River Basin Project. Under this project, workers built dams along the Missouri River. The project was designed to provide electricity, irrigation to croplands, and flood control. The dams also formed the Great Lakes of South Dakota, which have helped support the tourism industry.

Some of these lakes flooded Native American reservation farmland during the 1960s. As a result, disputes between Native Americans and the federal government resurfaced. Tensions between Native Americans and the government grew. In 1973 members of the American Indian Movement (AIM) took over Wounded Knee to protest government policies toward Native Americans. Three hundred people were arrested during the two and a half months of the takeover. Two Native Americans were killed.

In 1980 the United States Supreme Court ruled that the government must pay the Sioux $122.5 million for the Black Hills reservation land they lost in the 1870 gold rush. Most of the Sioux, however, demanded that instead of the money at least a million acres of land be returned. The issue has not yet been resolved.

In 1988 another drought swept over South Dakota farms, causing crop damage in the millions of dollars. The forests in the Black Hills were so dry that lightning started a wildfire. Nearly 17,000 acres were destroyed that July, and damages were again estimated in the millions of dollars.

Another disaster struck South Dakota in 1993 when the Missouri River flooded. The flood caused seven deaths in the state, and crop damage was estimated at about $7.5 million. That August, President Bill Clinton declared the flooded sections of the state disaster areas and approved an aid bill to provide over $12 billion in federal aid.

The people of South Dakota have proved themselves to be survivors. The state has been through booms, busts, droughts, and depressions. Through it all, however, South Dakota remains one of this country's great agricultural states.

During the 1973 occupation of Wounded Knee, an AIM protester celebrates the news that the federal government has agreed to extend its cease-fire for further talks.

Mr. Borglum's Big Idea

Gutzon Borglum sculpted many other works before beginning Mount Rushmore. One of his most famous is a bust of Abraham Lincoln, now kept in the United States Capitol.

Every year more than two million people travel to the Black Hills in South Dakota to see the Mount Rushmore National Memorial. The memorial is a huge sculpture of four presidential profiles carved into a granite mountain. Each head is about sixty feet high, or approximately the height of a six-story building.

The idea for a large-scale sculpture in the Black Hills began in 1923 with Doane Robinson, South Dakota's state historian. Robinson, however, originally had in mind a sculpture of Western folk heroes such as Buffalo Bill Cody, Lewis and Clark, Kit Carson, Sacajawea, and Chief Red Cloud. Robinson learned of a sculptor named Gutzon Borglum, who was known not only for creating uniquely "American" art, but also for designing that art on a grand scale. Robinson wrote to Borglum about the idea of sculpting a monument from a mountain face in the Black Hills. Borglum liked the idea and traveled to South Dakota to look for a location suitable for a gigantic

sculpture. He settled on a mountain that faced the southeast and caught the morning sunlight. That mountain was Mount Rushmore. Borglum's idea for the topic of the sculpture, however, was somewhat different from Doane Robinson's. Borglum wanted to honor four United States Presidents—George Washington, Thomas Jefferson, Theodore Roosevelt, and Abraham Lincoln.

Borglum, who had studied with the well-known French sculptor Auguste Rodin, began by making a detailed model of the four figures. He used a simple scale, in which one inch on the model represented one foot on the monument. Work began on Mount Rushmore in October 1927. Workers used dynamite to strip away tons of surface rock until they had exposed granite they could carve. Because of the nature of some of the rock, Borglum had to alter his model several times. He even had to relocate Jefferson's head when it was discovered that the granite in the original location wasn't suitable. The workers eventually perfected their blasting techniques so that they were able to get the features within a few inches of their finished measurements.

After blasting, workers used jackhammers to "honeycomb" the face of the rock with a network of carefully drilled holes. The holes weakened the rock, which workers could then pry off in sections. They used steel wedges to shape the figures' features. Finally, the rough surface of the sculpture was smoothed with an air gun until the granite had the texture of a city sidewalk. More than 350 people worked under Borglum's close supervision to create the memorial.

The project, which had been scheduled to last less than seven years, went on for twice that long. Much of the work was done during the Great Depression. Because the project created jobs and celebrated American history, Borglum and others were able to persuade the United States government to contribute almost all of the memorial's total cost of $989,992.32.

Borglum died in March 1941, but his son, Lincoln, supervised the project for another six months. Carving officially ceased in October 1941, shortly before the United States entered World War II. Many people don't realize that the memorial is unfinished—Borglum had always intended all four presidents to be full-figure statues.

Much of the work on Mount Rushmore involved fine detail, even though most people would see it only from a great distance.

When the construction of Mount Rushmore was first announced, one journalist called the idea as "ridiculous as keeping a cow in the rotunda of the Capitol."

Although Mount Rushmore was proclaimed a "Shrine of Democracy" at the 1930 dedication ceremony of Washington's head, not everyone sees it that way. The Lakota Sioux consider the area of the Black Hills, including Mount Rushmore, sacred. Some feel that the carving of the sculptures was a misuse of the land.

There is no doubt that, one way or another, Mount Rushmore has become an identifiable part of the American landscape. It's likely to remain so. Geologists, scientists that study rock, estimate that the monument will erode at a rate of about an

Borglum involved himself in every step of Mount Rushmore's construction.

inch every 1,500 years. In addition the National Park Service checks and repairs any cracks or other signs of erosion once a year. The natural strength of the rock combined with these preservation efforts will ensure that Mount Rushmore will stand as it looks now for many years.

These workers are sculpting one of Thomas Jefferson's eyes.

Gold in the Soil

The Black Hills gold rush, with its colorful characters and Wild West atmosphere, may be the most famous event in South Dakota's history. But it was farmers and ranchers, not miners, who built this state. South Dakota's economy remains largely agricultural.

In 1993 only four states had more land used for agriculture. South Dakota is the first in the nation in production of hay and rye. The state is among the top ten producers in the nation of most other major crops—including barley, oats, wheat, and sorghum. This is a lot of farm production from a state where the climate is severe. Temperatures can range from 110°F in the summer to –40°F in the winter. The soil is rich, but rainfall is uneven and unpredictable. Irrigation has helped stabilize conditions for many farmers. But life on the land can still be difficult in South Dakota.

About thirty percent of South Dakota's farming income comes from crops. The largest part—about sixty percent—comes from livestock. The ranches in the western part of the state provide grazing for cattle and

South Dakota is one of the leading producers of cattle in the United States.

Most of South Dakota's farmland is east of the Missouri River.

sheep. On some of these ranches, the work is still done on horseback in cowboy tradition. On other ranches pickups, helicopters, and other modern methods are used. In the eastern part of the state, the farmers raise hogs, chickens, and dairy cattle. In all, South Dakota livestock brought in over two billion dollars for the state in 1993.

If sixty percent of South Dakota's farm income comes from livestock and thirty percent comes from crops, what is the other ten percent? To help farmers, the federal government provides subsidies, or money grants. South Dakota receives about ten percent of its farm income from these subsidies. Most are for wheat and feed-grain farmers.

Clearly, the livelihoods of South Dakota's people are very much tied to the land. In fact, even manufacturing in South Dakota is connected to farms and farming. Manufacturing employs nearly forty thousand workers. Most of them work in food-processing plants,

In 1993 South Dakota livestock farmers raised nearly four million head of cattle.

packaging and preparing the many products of the state's agriculture industry. In addition, South Dakota's manufacturing growth in the early 1990s increased the salaries of the state's workers by the fifth highest rate in the nation.

The livestock from South Dakota's ranches are processed and packed in plants in Sioux Falls, Mitchell, Huron, and Rapid City. Fresh meat, canned meat, and hot dogs are some of South Dakota's livestock products. In addition, many people work in dairies, creameries, flour mills, and feed mills.

Wool is another important South Dakota livestock product. In fact, the town of Belle Fourche produces more wool than anyplace else in the nation.

South Dakota's next most important manufacturing activity is machinery. Machinery is also the state's most exported product. In 1993 machinery products brought in nearly $75 million in exports alone. Most of the machinery manufactured in the state is construction and farm equipment.

Manufacturing of electronic goods is one of the fastest-growing industries in the state. Manufacturers of personal computers and other products for the computer age are expanding, especially in urban areas such as Sioux Falls. South Dakota's businesses grew almost four times as fast as the rest of the nation in the early 1990s, largely because of development in the electronics industry.

Although the Black Hills gold rush ended, there's still enough gold left to be an important part of the economy. Mining accounts for about one percent of

above. In 1993 South Dakota poultry farmers raised about two and a half million turkeys.

below. Many people enjoy sailing in the South Dakota Great Lakes region, the area around the Missouri River in the middle of the state.

the total value of goods and services produced in the state. About half of that one percent comes from gold alone. In fact, the Homestake Mine in the heart of the Black Hills produces more gold than any other mine in the Western Hemisphere.

Petroleum, granite, sand, and gravel are also mined in South Dakota. Mining of zeolite, a mineral used mostly for soil and water treatment, has recently increased. Zeolite mining has especially helped the economy of some South Dakota Native American reservations, where zeolite is found.

Service industries are also important to South Dakota's economy. These are industries in which workers do not make a product but rather serve people or perform tasks for them. Service industries include so many different categories that, taken as a whole, they employ about three out of every four of South Dakota's workers. Most service workers in South Dakota—over sixty thousand in 1993—are employed in retail trade. Examples of jobs in retail trade are department store clerks, car salespeople, and restaurant servers.

The second most important category of service industries includes banks, insurance companies, and realtors. Almost twenty thousand of South Dakota's workers are employed in this category. Most of them work in Sioux Falls and Rapid City.

Many of South Dakota's service industry workers are involved in the tourist industry, one of the state's

Miners test soil for gold by panning. They place dirt in a pan, add water, then swirl the pan until the gold, which is heavier than the soil, separates out.

most important sources of income. In 1994 alone, visitors spent nearly five hundred million dollars in South Dakota. Tourists streamed in to see natural sites, such as the Badlands and the Black Hills, and human-made monuments, such as Mount Rushmore and the Crazy Horse Memorial. On average, the number of visitors increases by about ten percent each year, and there's no sign of a future decline.

South Dakota is particularly proud of its economic success because of the difficulties it has had in the past. But all of its products—from grains to machinery to natural beauty—are in high demand. Even if things slow down, the people of South Dakota have already proved that they can weather the changes.

Nature's Way Is Best

Hundreds of years ago, the Great Plains of South Dakota were almost entirely covered with grass. Native Americans grew a few crops, but they did not grow enough to affect the grasslands very much.

The thousands of kinds of grasses that grew on the Great Plains were good for the soil. The native grasses were strong enough to survive South Dakota's harsh, windy weather. The grass also protected the soil from being carried away by wind and water. Buffalo and other animals ate the grass and helped turn over the soil by churning it with their hooves. When the grass died and decayed, its nutrients returned to the soil.

When farmers came to the plains, they replaced the native grasses with food crops such as wheat and corn. Unfortunately those early farmers used methods that harmed South Dakota's soil. When they harvested their corn and wheat, they removed most of the plant. They even removed the stubble left after the harvest, so none of the plant was left to decay and add nutrients to the soil. Meanwhile, the soil was left exposed to the wind and rain.

Because of these problems, South Dakota lost valuable soil. Unprotected topsoil was blown away by wind or washed away by water. This process is called erosion.

South Dakota's farmers know better now. Today, they are trying new methods to conserve the soil. One method farmers use to prevent erosion is contour farming. Instead of planting square fields, farmers plant in curved patterns that follow the natural slope

Modern farming methods have improved South Dakota's corn crops over the years.

Leaving plant stubble in the field helps to ensure a healthy crop for the following year.

of the land. Contour farming helps reduce erosion from water runoff.

Some plants protect the soil from wind erosion better than others, so farmers may alternate row by row between crops that protect the soil better and crops that protect it less.

South Dakota farmers also rotate crops, which means that they plant a different crop in the same field each year. Different plants use different nutrients from the soil, so crop rotation helps keep the soil from losing too much of any one nutrient. Once a crop is harvested, farmers leave the plant stubble on the field to decay and replenish the soil.

Since the 1930s farmers have developed hardier strains of wheat and corn that are suited to South Dakota's weather. However, farmers may have to replant stronger native grasses in places to conserve the soil.

Nature has taught South Dakota farmers a harsh lesson. Now with the aid of modern farming techniques,

Wheat is only one of the seven thousand types of grasses that exist worldwide.

farmers can help the land renew itself. This ensures healthier soil, which means healthier crops for the farmers in South Dakota.

Art on
the Frontier

In the late 1800s, many immigrants from Europe streamed into South Dakota. They came with years of farming experience, and they were anxious to apply their talents to the fertile South Dakota land. Families that are descended from these immigrants add German, Russian, Czechoslovakian, and Scandinavian touches to South Dakota's cultural life.

The work of Norwegian-born writer Ole Edvart Rölvaag is one of the best examples of South Dakota's cultural richness. Rölvaag spent his early years near Sioux Falls in the southeastern part of the state. His famous 1924 novel, *Giants in the Earth*, is about the struggles faced by the Norwegian farmers in the area. Throughout his life, Rölvaag encouraged all immigrants on the frontier to enrich their new nation by holding on to their cultural heritage.

The people with perhaps the strongest cultural heritage in South Dakota have been there for centuries—the Native Americans. One of South Dakota's—and the nation's—best-known Native

This man will dust himself off and try another time at the Oglala Nation Rodeo on the Pine Ridge Reservation. In saddle bronc riding, the rider must stay on the horse for eight seconds.

Built in 1892, the Mitchell Corn Palace is redecorated every fall in murals that are made of corn and other grains in a variety of colors. Concerts, dances, and other community events are held in the building.

American artists is Oscar Howe, a Yankton Sioux. Howe is best known for his use of traditional Sioux symbols in his paintings. His most unique projects were for the Corn Palace in Mitchell, South Dakota. The outside walls of the Corn Palace are decorated with scenes made entirely of corn and grains. Howe began designing these scenes in 1948, and he created a new set every year for nearly 25 years. Howe served as South Dakota's artist laureate for more than 25 years, until his death in 1983.

South Dakota also had a famous poet laureate, Charles Badger Clark, from 1937 until his death in 1957. Clark was one of the first acclaimed "cowboy poets," writing about life on the range. Clark's home in the Black Hills is now part of Custer State Park. A walking trail has been cleared on his former property, and signs carrying his poetry mark the route.

Another pioneer artist was Harvey Dunn. The son of South Dakota homesteaders, Dunn first became famous for his illustrations in the *Saturday Evening Post* in the early 1900s. Dunn later found acclaim for his paintings of frontier life.

Some of the state's richest resources are its community and summer theaters. The Black Hills Playhouse has presented summer theater in Custer State Park since 1946. South Dakota has a symphony orchestra, which also hosts opera companies. One of the newest cultural additions to the state is the Civic Dance Association near Sioux Falls.

South Dakota's natural landscape—enhanced by human contributions such as the Mount Rushmore and Crazy Horse monuments—is the most breathtaking aspect of the state's culture. Almost 1,500 buffalo wander in the 73,000 acres of Custer State Park. In the Badlands National Park, the landscape takes on the appearance of the moon's surface! The Badlands display the astonishing effects of more than 37 million years of erosion on miles of sandstone and clay soils. In the northern part of the state, the more level land along the upper Missouri River provided beautiful scenery for the movie *Dances with Wolves*.

In some ways the land has made things difficult for its inhabitants. But it has also given much in return. The natural landscape, along with the art, music, and literature inspired by its beauty, has helped to create a distinctive culture in South Dakota.

The cowboy tradition is kept alive in South Dakota by rodeos. Most of the state's rodeos take place in July and August.

This painting by Harvey Dunn is called "After School."

Powwow—
Celebration of Life

The term *powwow* comes from the Algonquin word *pau wau*. A pau wau is a healer or spiritual leader. Pau waus sometimes performed religious dances, so early European explorers in the areas where Algonquins lived thought that *pau wau* was the name of the dance.

Today, powwows are community as well as religious events that include dancing, drumming, singing, and socializing. The purpose of a powwow is to make sure that Native Americans' histories, cultures, and traditions are not forgotten. Native Americans have been holding this kind of powwow for about one hundred years.

One group of Sioux living in South Dakota is the Lakota. People from many states come to Lakota powwows, and Lakota people also go

This child is wearing a dress decorated with cone-shaped bells for the jingle dress dance. If a dancer doesn't keep in time with the drums, the judges can tell from the jingling of the bells.

Eagle feathers have long been a part of the ceremonial dress of many Native Americans. Now Native Americans must obtain a permit to gather the feathers because many eagles are endangered species.

to powwows in other places. That way, people from different areas share their traditions with each other.

The "giveaway" is sometimes part of a powwow. The person sponsoring the giveaway calls his or her friends out of the crowd to give them gifts, such as blankets, shawls, and money. The host of a giveaway may also give people gifts as a way of asking them to be friends.

"It goes back to the custom of generosity among the Lakota people," explained Frank Dillon, a reporter for a Lakota newspaper. "Long ago our head men and our chiefs . . . acquired wealth as leaders—acquired horses, acquired a lot of buffalo robes. . . . The leader, to show that he's a leader, would give all this away." The leader would, however, keep a horse or two.

A leader has to be practical as well as generous.

All powwows include music and dancing. Dancing is one way for the Lakota to celebrate the survival of their culture. Dances can tell stories, or they can teach about nature. Like other Native Americans, the Lakota respect nature. Many Lakota dances imitate animals and natural forces, such as the wind and the sun. Dancing shows appreciation for nature. Dancing also helps Lakotas to teach their children about their history.

"The powwow is an important expression of our culture, the Lakota culture. . . ." said Dillon. "It gives people a chance to talk to one another and just get together . . . for the love of being together in a powwow."

Powwows are an important Native American family event. Children are especially encouraged to participate, to ensure that traditions are passed on to younger generations.

The Return of Crazy Horse

Crazy Horse, a Lakota Sioux, is one of the most famous Native Americans in history. For many years the Sioux had lived in the area that is now South Dakota. But when European settlers arrived in the area, they often came into conflict with the Native Americans. In 1874 the United States government wanted to take the Black Hills because gold had been discovered there. A treaty had been signed in 1868 by President Andrew Johnson that said, "As long as rivers run and grass grows and trees bear leaves, Paha Sapa [the Black Hills] will forever be the sacred land of the Sioux. . . ." Later the government ignored that treaty and began trying to force the Sioux to leave.

The United States government sent army troops to fight the Sioux, but the Sioux defended their territory. At the famous Battle of the Little Bighorn, Crazy Horse and his followers defeated the United States troops. The Sioux hoped that the victory had earned them peace. However, the United States Army continued to attack the Sioux. In 1877 Crazy Horse and his followers could hold out no longer, and they surrendered. Crazy Horse was imprisoned. He was killed a few months after his surrender, probably while trying to escape.

Sadly, the treatment of all groups of Native Americans in the 1800s included broken treaties and loss of native lands. By the twentieth century,

Korczak poses here with a model of the Crazy Horse Memorial. Before beginning the monument, Korczak helped to carve Mount Rushmore.

This scale model of the Crazy Horse Memorial weighs 16 tons, but it is still 34 times smaller than the statue will be. The monument, in the process of being sculpted, is in the background.

many non-Native American people had come to recognize that the United States had treated the Native Americans harshly and unfairly. One person who felt strongly about what had happened to Native Americans was a sculptor named Korczak Ziolkowski.

Back in 1940 Korczak, who was known simply by his first name, received an invitation from Lakota Sioux Chief Henry Standing Bear to create a sculpture of Crazy Horse from a mountain in the Black Hills. Korczak made a model for the memorial that showed the brave warrior seated proudly upon his stallion and pointing boldly toward the land of his people.

Korczak felt that Crazy Horse's will and determination to fight for his peoples' land represented all Native Americans' struggle to keep their heritage.

In 1947 Korczak began the huge project. He insisted that the memorial should receive no money from the United States government. Instead the memorial would be funded by donations from visitors and others who supported the project. Even though he received offers that could have meant several million dollars in federal funds, he refused them.

For the first five years of the project, Korczak worked almost entirely alone. Much of the initial work involved removing tons of granite with

Crazy Horse's face is scheduled for completion in 1998.

dynamite. He used a jackhammer drill to do more detailed shaping. Most of the shaping techniques were similar to those that workers had used on Mount Rushmore, another huge monument. Mount Rushmore had been carved from another mountain just 17 miles away.

As the years passed, some rough features of Crazy Horse became more visible in the granite. In 1951 Korczak painted a white outline on the mountain face to help visitors "see" what the finished sculpture would look like. By 1961 more than one million tons of rock had been removed and the beginnings of Crazy Horse's head and arm came into view. For the next twenty or so years, blasting and drilling continued. Korczak also worked on detailed plans about how each part of the sculpture would be carved.

In 1982 Korczak died. He had always known that the project would not be completed in his lifetime. All of Korczak's ten children and his wife had contributed over the years to the project. Korczak taught some of them how to remove and carve the stone to create the monument. His wife and most of his children have promised to continue Korczak's work on the memorial until it is complete.

Korczak left three books of plans and measurements so that his family could go forward with the project. In the 1990s carving that was done on Crazy Horse's eyes, eyelids, nose, and cheeks helped bring the statue to life.

When finished, the Crazy Horse Memorial will be the largest statue in the world. The entire Mount Rushmore monument, which is composed of four sixty-foot-high Presidents' heads, is smaller than Crazy Horse's head alone, which is about ninety feet high!

A less obvious but extremely important part of Korczak's long-range plan involved his commitment to making the memorial serve an educational purpose. Parts of that plan have already been achieved. Near the memorial, Korczak and his sons built the Indian Museum of North America. Since the early 1970s, people at the museum have taught visitors about Native American history and culture. The museum has three large exhibit halls and holds more than twenty thousand examples of Native American art. Korczak also planned to establish a university and medical training center for Native Americans. The university will be funded by admission fees from the memorial. Presently the Crazy Horse Memorial finances scholarships for Native American college students by setting aside some of the entrance fees collected from the more than one million people who visit the Crazy Horse Memorial each year.

The progress on the Crazy Horse Memorial continues, but it's impossible to predict when the largest statue in the world will be finished. The Ziolkowski family, however, is determined to carry out the sculptor's dream of building an educational and cultural memorial to Native Americans.

The Ziolkowski family has dedicated themselves to finishing the monument, which will be taller than the pyramids of Egypt and the Washington Monument.

A Future on the Frontier

When you look at the future of South Dakota, it helps to remember that it is still a very young state. It just celebrated its hundredth birthday in 1989. At a time when many other states are trying to correct past mistakes that have resulted in pollution, overcrowding, and waste of natural and human resources, South Dakota is working with a nearly clean slate.

In agriculture, great progress has been made in irrigating the land. Over three hundred thousand acres of barren land in South Dakota have been made into profitable farmland. Better farming methods continue to be developed. Although farmers are still struggling, they have definite hope for the future.

The future appears less hopeful, however, for the people with the longest history in South Dakota—the Native Americans. Recent court rulings have acknowledged that South Dakota's Sioux deserve compensation for the land taken from them by the American government. But acknowledgment is not enough. The many Sioux groups of South Dakota are fighting to

The falls of the Big Sioux River gave the nearby city of Sioux Falls its name. South Dakota's fresh air and plentiful water make the state inviting to people and businesses.

Pioneers in wagon trains had one rule: "Keep moving." The motto is still appropriate to South Dakota today, as it moves into the twenty-first century.

regain lost land. Also, conditions on Native American reservations are poor. Some reservations have unemployment rates as high as seventy percent. They need help improving education, health services, and job-training programs. The more than fifty thousand Native Americans in South Dakota are crucial to the state's identity. They need government recognition that matches their importance.

What South Dakota desperately needs—for all its inhabitants—are jobs. Too many people now leave the state to look for employment. Recent business growth has helped, however. Citibank Corporation, one of the largest financial institutions in the world, has moved its national headquarters to Sioux Falls. In addition, manufacturing has boomed in the state, expanding by as much as ten percent each year in the early 1990s.

It will be interesting to see whether South Dakota can avoid the mistakes, especially environmental ones, made by so many other states. The people of South Dakota are doing their best to maintain a solid base for the future of their frontier state.

Important Historical Events

500 The Mound Builders civilization begins in the South Dakota area along the Missouri River.

1682 The South Dakota area is claimed for France as part of the Louisiana Territory.

1743 The La Vérendrye brothers explore the South Dakota region.

1803 The United States buys the Louisiana Territory, which includes South Dakota, from France.

1804 Meriwether Lewis and William Clark stop in South Dakota on their way to the Pacific Ocean.

1817 Joseph La Framboise establishes the first permanent European settlement in South Dakota at present-day Fort Pierre.

1823 Native Americans attempt to block a trading party traveling up the Missouri, killing 13 American traders.

1861 The Dakota Territory is created.

1868 Red Cloud's War over the Bozeman Trail ends after two years of fighting, and the Great Sioux Reservation is created by the Fort Laramie Treaty.

1876 Lieutenant Colonel George Custer and all his troops are killed at the Battle of Little Bighorn in Montana, as the Sioux fight to keep their land.

1878 to 1887 Settlers flood into the state during the Great Dakota Land Boom.

1889 On November 2, South Dakota becomes the fortieth state.

1890 The massacre at Wounded Knee Creek marks the end of serious fighting between settlers and Native Americans in the area.

1890s A severe drought cripples farming.

1911 Another drought hits South Dakota.

1927 Gutzon Borglum begins work on Mount Rushmore.

1930s The Great Depression and another major drought falls upon the state.

1946 A project to build dams along the Missouri River, providing electricity, flood control, and irrigation, begins.

1948 Korczak Ziolkowski begins work on the Crazy Horse Memorial.

1973 The village of Wounded Knee is taken over by Native Americans in protest against government policies.

1980 The Supreme Court rules that the United States government owes the Sioux over $120 million. The Sioux refuse the offer because instead of money they want their land back.

1988 Yet another severe drought hits South Dakota, hurting farmers and causing a devastating fire in the Black Hills.

1993 Flooding on the Missouri River ruins many South Dakota crops. President Bill Clinton declares parts of the state disaster areas and provides aid to farmers.

Around the seal on South Dakota's state flag is a gold border that represents the sun. The riverboat, pictured on the Missouri River, represents trade and transportation. The smelting furnace represents mining. The grazing cattle and the farmer planting the corn field represent agriculture.

South Dakota Almanac

Nicknames. The Mount Rushmore State, the Sunshine State, the Land of Infinite Variety

Capital. Pierre

State Bird. Ring-necked pheasant

State Flower. American pasqueflower

State Tree. Black Hills spruce

State Motto. Under God the People Rule

State Song. "Hail, South Dakota"

State Abbreviations. S. Dak. (traditional); SD (postal)

Statehood. November 2, 1889, the fortieth state

Government. Congress: U.S. senators, 2; U.S. representatives, 1. State Legislature: senators, 35; representatives, 70. Counties: 66

Area. 77,122 sq mi (199,744 sq km), 16th in size among the states

Greatest Distances. north/south, 237 mi (382 km); east/west, 383 mi (617 km)

Elevation. Highest: Harney Peak, 7,242 ft (2,207 m). Lowest: Big Stone Lake, 962 ft (293 m)

Population. 1990 Census: 699,999 (1% increase over 1980), 45th among the states. Density: 9 persons per sq mi (4 persons per sq km). Distribution: 50% urban, 50% rural. 1980 Census: 690,768

Economy. *Agriculture:* beef and dairy cattle, sheep, hay, rye, barley, oats, wheat, sorghum, hogs. *Manufacturing:* food products, machinery, electronics, precision instruments. *Mining:* gold, granite, sand and gravel, zeolite

State Seal

State Bird: Ring-necked pheasant

State Flower: American pasqueflower

Annual Events

★ Snow Queen Festival in Aberdeen (January)

★ Schmeckfest in Freeman (March)

★ Laura Ingalls Wilder Pageant in De Smet (June)

★ Black Hills and Northern Plains Indian Powwow in Rapid City (July)

★ Sitting Bull Stampede Rodeo in Mobridge (July)

★ Deadwood Gold Rush Days of '76 (August)

★ State Fair in Huron (August)

★ Corn Palace Festival in Mitchell (September)

★ Crazy Horse Mountain Carving Night Blast, near Custer (September)

★ Ugly Vehicle Contest in Miller (October)

Places to Visit

★ Badlands National Park, near the Black Hills

★ Black Hills National Forest and Custer State Park

★ Corn Palace in Mitchell

★ Cosmos Mystery Area, near Rapid City

★ Crazy Horse Memorial, near Custer

★ Cultural Heritage Center in Pierre

★ Deadwood in the Black Hills

★ Laura Ingalls Wilder Memorial in De Smet

★ Mount Rushmore National Memorial in the Black Hills

★ Prehistoric Indian Village, at Lake Mitchell

★ Shrine to Music Museum in Vermillion

★ Wall Drug Store in Wall

47

Index